Christmas Trees

CHRISTMAS TREES

Fun and Festive Ideas

by Peter Cole, Frankie Frankeny,
and Leslie Jonath

CHRONICLE BOOKS
SAN FRANCISCO

Library of Congress Cataloging-in-Publication Data available.

ISBN: 0-8118-3577-4

Manufactured in China

Food Styling by Diane Gsell
Book Design by Laura Lovett
Typeset in FF Scala, Pixie, Viva, and Hoffmann

Distributed in Canada by Raincoast Books
9050 Shaughnessy Street
Vancouver, British Columbia V6P 6E5

10 9 8 7 6 5 4 3 2 1

Chronicle Books LLC
85 Second Street
San Francisco, California 94105

www.chroniclebooks.com

Acknowledgments

For sharing not only their crafting genius and creative ideas but also their generous Christmas spirit every day of the year, we especially want to thank Jarka Kavinova, Camella Haeker, and Elise Cannon. For bringing her festive Christmas cookies, cupcakes, and other treats to our holiday table, we thank Diane Gsell.

At Chronicle Books, we are grateful to our editors, Mikyla Bruder and Jodi Davis, for helping us to make the book come to life with magic! For making the book look a lot like Christmas, we are also grateful to Laura Lovett. For her expert book development advice and help, we would like to thank Sharon Silva.

Special thanks also to Arielle Eckstut, Lindsay Anderson, Julianne Balmain, Jean von Brockdorf of Meadow Vista Tree Farm & Nursery, Alexandra C. Cole, Wendy and Eli Mardigian-Des Jardins, Dan Geller, Dayna Goldfine, Monica, Hannalore and Guenther Heineman, Sam Kraus, Zach Kraus, Anton Krukowski, Maxi and Eric Lilly, John Mark, Bill Norman, Derek Piper, Chance Piper, Michael and Ivy Ruggiero, Mattie Shelton, Wolfgang Molke of Red Desert Cactus, Noel Christmas Tree Farm, and Elizabeth Takeuchi.

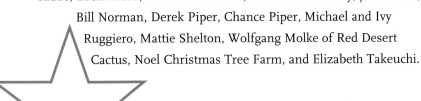

Contents

Introduction

"O Christmas tree, O Christmas tree, how lovely are your branches!" Nothing signals the beginning of the Christmas season like choosing and decorating the tree. From the tough decision of picking out the ideal candidate (small and bushy? tall and slender?) and getting it home (on the car? behind the sleigh?) to hanging the lights, draping the tinsel, and tussling over the ornaments (who gets to top the tree with the fluffy pink angel?), trimming the tree has been a beloved tradition for over four hundred years, with origins that date back much earlier.

Long before the celebration of Christmas, evergreen trees were thought to have mystical powers. Gorgeously vibrant in winter while other trees stood bare, evergreens were hopeful symbols of life and fertility. Friendly spirits were said to hide in the branches, and small trees or cut boughs were brought indoors to act as lucky charms. The Romans hung evergreen branches in their homes and temples during the solstice in honor of Saturn, the god of agriculture, to remind them of the greenery that would come again when spring returned.

Many wonderful stories and legends surround how the decorated Christmas tree came to be. One story describes how the world's most colorful flowers and trees, each wearing its most vibrant bloom, came to see the baby Jesus on the night of his birth. The evergreen tree was embarrassed to have neither colorful leaves nor flowers. Feeling sorry for the tree, some of the stars descended from the sky to sparkle on its branches.

Another legend credits Martin Luther, a founder of the Protestant Church, with beginning the tradition when late one winter evening, he noticed how beautifully the stars shone through the trees. To share this magic moment with his wife, he carried a tree home, where he placed small, lighted candles on the branches to re-create the starry Christmas sky.

We know for sure that evergreens were decorated in the Middle Ages when miracle plays were used to teach the lessons of the Bible. The Paradise Play, which showed the fall of Adam and Eve, called for a Tree of Knowledge full of luscious fruit. Because the play was performed in winter, when most fruit trees were bare, an evergreen hung with shiny red apples was used instead.

At about the same time in Germany, the *Lichtstock,* or light stick, a small pyramid-like frame topped with a candle, became very popular. Also known as the Christmas light, this simple construction symbolized the birth of Christ as the light of the world. Evergreen branches were wound around each leg of the pyramid and a star or a pinecone graced the top. On the day before Christmas, some German families stood a glowing *Lichtstock* beside a decorated evergreen. In time, people came to combine the two traditions: The candles of the *Lichtstock* were attached to the boughs of the evergreen, and the star was taken from the apex of the pyramid and placed on the top of the fir. In this way, the Christmas tree as we know it today was born.

Early tree trimmers added bright paper roses, stars, and snowflakes; gilded nuts; apples; and homemade treats such as honey cakes, gingerbread, and sugared fruits. In 1870, glass ornaments known as *kugels* were added, blown in fabulous shapes from tiny trumpets to painted vases, silver foil icicles, shiny elephants, banjos, and locomotives. While some early Scrooges said, "Bah humbug" to these frivolous displays at Christmastime, the tree itself was so enchanting that the custom soon caught on in Finland, Denmark, Norway, and France. Queen Victoria's German husband, Prince Albert, brought the native German tradition to England, where he put up the first royal Christmas tree in Windsor Castle in 1848. The tree became an English sensation, a Victorian symbol laden with ornaments and surrounded with gifts. The tradition of decorating a tree at Christmas also traveled with the earliest German immigrants to the United States and Canada, where in 1882 a fir was first strung with electric lights. Since then, outdoor Christmas trees have lit up the night all over the world.

There are as many ways to trim a tree as there are stars in the sky. Indeed, a decorated tree is as individual as a snowflake. If you are like most Christmas season enthusiasts, you may already have your own treasure trove of trimming traditions. But why stop there? Let the Christmas spirit inspire you to have more fun and more trees. As the old saying goes, "The more the merrier!"

In *Christmas Trees*, we present a forest full of ideas to spread holiday cheer. We've drawn on traditions from around the world and have also shared a few wacky ones of our own.

Chapter 1 will help you choose a tree and get started with the decorations. Chapter 2 offers projects and ideas for decorating freshly cut or live trees, and Chapter 3 concentrates on holiday trees that don't require a real tree at all. Chapter 4 includes a few edible trees and some holiday treats for your tree-trimming party. Throughout the book, we give instructions on how to tackle the trimming, but you don't need to follow our sleigh down the slope. Feel free to use our ideas as guidelines, and then go ahead and carve out your own path.

So put on some Nat King Cole, Elvis, or Bing, fill your cookie plates with sugarplums, and start decorating a tree. Although it's been said many times, with many trees, Merry Christmas to you!

Tree-Trimming Traditions from Around the World

☆ In England, Victorian Christmas trees were cluttered with penny toys. Especially popular were toys with wheels: trucks and trains and pull toys in the shapes of lambs and horses and other animals. The Victorians also hung little cardboard shoes filled with sweets and scented wadding on their trees. One of the shoes would contain a ring, making it the lucky shoe. After Christmas dinner, the girls in the family would choose a shoe from the tree. The girl who got the one with the ring was destined to be the first to marry.

☆ In Scandinavia, simple straw stars and cute billy goats adorn Christmas trees.

☆ In Denmark, trees are decorated with woven basket hearts and little Jule-nissen. The Jule-nissen dress like little leprechauns in red hats. The nissen love children and cats and bring good luck into the house but can be very unruly if not fed properly. (If you have Jule-nissen on your tree, be sure to leave a bowl of porridge to keep them happy.)

☆ In Eastern Europe, glass fruit and vegetables adorn the tree. Most glass ornaments were hand-blown in Lauscha, Germany. In Germany, the parents hung a pickle deep in the tree. Whoever found the pickle would receive an extra gift from St Nick. Now, glass pickles keep the tradition alive!

☆ In Norway, sailors were said to have tied a tree to the mast of every ship sailing under the national flag. Traditionally, Norwegian parents decorate the Christmas tree in secret. Once the sparkling tree is revealed to the children, everyone joins hands around the tree and sings carols.

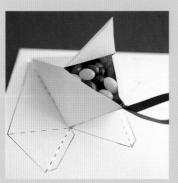

☆ In early-twentieth-century America, ornaments made of paper and papier-mâché were especially popular. Candy-filled papier-mâché fish and cornucopias delighted children and adults alike.

☆ In Mexico, a bare tree branch is collected from the countryside and hung with small piñatas and other bright, colorful folk art.

☆ In the Philippines, colorful handmade trees hold star lanterns made from bamboo sticks and rice paper or cellophane and tassels.

chapter one

☆ Terrific Trees

Choosing a Tree

When it comes to picking out a fresh tree, you might already have a favorite type. Some people like tall, narrow trees, while others prefer their trees squat and plump. In every case, however, your final selection will have certain characteristics—color, smell, needle size, branch size, and needle retention—that differ from one type of tree to the next. Some trees have long needles, some short. Some are very fragrant, and some are decidedly subtle. Some shed their needles like reindeer shed their antlers while others keep their needles long after the holiday season has passed.

Buying a tree requires some planning. First, consider the height of your ceilings and the scale of your room. Obviously, a ten-foot white pine calls for a huge room, while a beautiful bonsai might be just the tree for a tiny apartment alcove. Allow at least a foot of clearance between the top of the tree and the ceiling. Before putting the tree in its final location, lay a heavy sheet of plastic to protect the floor or surface on which the tree will stand. If you have the space consider a small potted tree. In addition to holiday cheer, a living tree can be decorated year after year. Check with your local nursery for the best trees for your region and their care.

If you are cutting your tree at a farm, take along a pair of gloves, a tape measure, a blanket, a rope, and a saw. If you are choosing from precut trees, test the tree for freshness by hitting the trunk to see how many needles fall off. Transport the tree home inside your car if possible. If you have to put it on your car, wrap it in an old blanket and secure it tightly with rope. When you get your tree home, place it immediately in a tree stand and give it water.

Tree Stands and Skirts

The most important consideration when choosing a stand is how much water it will hold. A good rule of thumb is one quart for every inch in diameter of the tree's trunk. You should also make sure that the stand fits the tree—if it is too big or too small, it might end up tipping over. Do not trim the sides of the trunk to fit it in a stand as trees drink from the sides near the trunk, and removing them will inhibit the tree's water intake. Before inserting the tree into the tree stand, make a cut about a half inch deep or more across the base of the trunk. Place the tree in the stand and add water immediately. Standing a tree in water will keep it fresh and more fire resistant. Add water to the stand every two or three days.

If you don't already have a festive tree skirt to wrap around the trunk, use a large rectangle of thick fabric, such as felt, to catch falling needles. You can buy felt at most fabric stores.

A Few Great Evergreens

Although your tree will most likely be a pine, spruce, fir,
or cedar, the variety of tree will vary from region to region.
Here are just a few of the most commonly available varieties:

Balsam fir: *Fir branches are airier than those of pines or spruces.*
Their short, flat, long-lasting, dark green needles are very fragrant.

Colorado blue spruce: *The blue spruce has short, powdery blue, prickly*
needles that grow bottle-brush style on the branches and scare off cats.

Douglas fir: *The short, dark green needles grow in rows, giving this*
tree a feathery look. The thin branches are not good for heavy ornaments.

Eastern white pine: *With exceptionally long hairlike needles of 2 to*
5 inches, this tree has a unique soft character. The tightly bunched
branches don't showcase the ornaments as well as those of firs do.

Fraser fir: *Said to have the best needle retention, the Fraser fir is*
beloved for the silvery underside of its needles that contrast with the dark
green on top.

Scotch pine: *Pleasantly fragrant with a gorgeous red-orange bark, the*
Scotch pine has sturdy branches perfect for hanging heavy ornaments.

White fir or concolor fir: *This fragrant, bell-shaped tree has blue-*
green needles 1/2 to 1 1/2 inches long and holds its needles well.

White pine: *If you like a tree with a subtle fragrance, this might be*
the one for you. Long-lasting, with blue-green needles 2 to 5 inches long
and little fragrance, this is the largest pine in the United States.

White spruce: *This chubby tree has airy branches and green to*
bluish needles 1/2 to 3/4 inch long.

Lights, Candles, Action!

Many people think that in the old days, candles blazed on trees throughout the twelve days of Christmas, but in truth they were lit for no more than half an hour at a time. Because the threat of fire was great, buckets of water to douse minor blazes were hidden in the room where the tree stood. Lit candles should never be used on trees. Instead, use them on your holiday table to create that seasonal glow.

It wasn't long after Thomas Edison invented the electric lightbulb that Christmas enthusiasts strung a few together to ring around the tree. Since that time, tree-lighting ceremonies have delighted people from Rockefeller Center to Trafalgar Square. Now you can buy lights in all shapes and sizes and in all colors of the rainbow, as well as lights that twinkle, blink, and beep. We've used simple lights for the theme trees in this book, but you can substitute whatever turns you and your tree on. String the lights on your tree first before adding any other decoration, and make sure that the cords are not frayed in any way.

Homemade Ornaments and Tree Toppers

You don't have to be a crafter to make beautiful, whimsical ornaments and tree toppers. And you don't need to buy lots of high-priced supplies. Many of the projects in this book were made from everyday materials. Check your closets and drawers and local flea markets for inexpensive stuff that you can fashion into ornaments. Take a second look at that collection of buttons, stamps, beads, pet toys, playing cards, or old plastic cars. With a little hot glue, you can turn anything into a tree-trimming treasure.

Tools for Santa's Tree-Trimming Elves

Just as Santa's elves have tools to make toys, the following tools and materials will be useful to have in your Christmas workshop:

Christmas balls in a range of colors and sizes
Christmas lights
Christmas music (to listen to while working)
Construction paper
Extension cords, indoor and outdoor
Flexible metal wire
Floral wire
Glitter
Glue (hot glue, white glue, spray adhesive)
Hammers
Handsaws
Ornament hangers

Paint (acrylic, latex, fluorescent, spray paint)
Paintbrushes in various sizes
Pipe cleaners
Pliers
Poster board
Scissors
Tape (masking, electrical, clear)
Tinsel
Twine
Utility knife
Wooden stakes (for outdoor trees)
Wire cutters
X-Acto knife
Xmas spirit

Fire Safety

Trees do not cause fires; trees catch fire.
You can prevent fires by taking the following
precautions:

☆ *Place your tree away from heat registers,*
space heaters, fireplaces, wood stoves, televisions,
and other heat sources.

☆ *Keep your tree stand filled with water.*

☆ *Check lights and electrical decorations*
for wear. Do not use lights or appliances with
frayed cords. Use only UL-approved electrical
decorations and extension cords.

☆ *Never use candles on the tree.*

☆ *Unplug tree lights and other decorations*
when you're out of the room or sleeping.

Artificial Christmas Trees

Toward the end of the 1800s, artificial trees were made of wire skeletons that were covered with goose, turkey, ostrich, or swan feathers. The feathers were often dyed green to imitate pine needles. In 1930, the Addis Brush company created the first artificial brush tree. The Addis "silver pine" tree was patented in 1950. Today, many different kinds of artificial trees are sold, including realistic natural-looking trees. Most of the projects in this book call for real trees, but their artificial counterparts can have a beauty all their own.

Remove and Recycle

In some Scandinavian countries, people leave their trees up until January 13, which is known as King Knut's Day, after an early Norse ruler. On this, the last day of the Christmas season, the tree is stripped of its ornaments and carried out of the house as the family sings "Twenty days of Knut, we dance the tree out."

Whatever your tree-removing ritual, you can recycle a fresh tree. If you don't want to mulch the tree yourself, contact your local recycling authority to find out how you can safely dispose of it. Dry trees are extremely flammable, so dispose of the tree soon after the holidays. To get the tree out of the house without scattering needles throughout the rooms, simply cut off the branches with pruning shears over a drop cloth while the tree is still in its stand. Do not burn the tree in your fireplace as the resin from the needles can clog your chimney. (And then how would Santa get into your house next year?)

Baked Dough Ornaments

2 cups all-purpose flour
1/2 cup salt
1 heaping tablespoon
    nontoxic powdered
    tempera paint
approximately 3/4 cup
    water
ornament wires

Here's an easy recipe for making ornaments. Make separate batches of dough for each desired color. It is best to use the dough within 4 hours.

 Preheat the oven to 300°F.

In a large bowl, mix together the flour, salt, and tempera. Add the water gradually, mixing thoroughly with both hands to make a stiff but not sticky dough. If the dough feels too stiff to work, add a bit more water.

Turn the dough out onto a nonstainable surface and knead it for 3 to 5 minutes. If the dough seems too soft, sprinkle a little flour on the table and knead it in. To make ornaments, place dough on paper towels, and use knives, forks, and skewers to shape the dough. A garlic press can be used to make angel hair. Press ornament wires into dough before baking.

To bake, place ornaments on nonstick or foil-lined baking sheets. Bake for 2 to 2 1/2 hours, or until firm. Remove the ornaments from the baking sheets while still hot to prevent sticking. Cool completely on a rack.

Very Merry Christmas Trees

Although you might already have your favorite tried and true traditions, we invite you to take a look these new twists on Christmas themes. Here are crazy ideas for trees, inside and out—using all trees both great and small. We've specified the ideal size tree for each project, but you can always improvise to use what you have on hand.

Santa Tree

You will need:

1 bushy tree, 6 to 8 feet tall,
  in a sturdy tree stand
1 yard red felt
1 clay pot, large enough to
  accomodate the tree
  stand, painted black
20 to 30 safety pins
1 large bag (5 pounds) polyester stuffing
scissors
1 strip black felt, 2 yards
  long by 6 inches wide
2 small blue Christmas
  balls, with hangers
about 60 red ornaments,
  in all sizes and shapes,
  with hangers (see page
  31)

Yes, Virginia, there is a Santa Claus.

Although Santa is hard to catch sight of, with faith and a little crafting expertise, you will prove the skeptics wrong. Santa Claus was born in the Middle Ages. Before Saint Nick had his current job at the North Pole, he was already famous for his generosity and kindness and the miracles he performed for children and the poor.

To make Santa, you will need about 60 red orna- ments. You can find polyester stuffing at most fabric stores. We glued a glittery belt buckle to a black strip of felt to spice up his outfit and gave him a pair of sparkly spectacles.

☆ Fit the base of the tree (in the tree stand) in the clay pot. You may have to clip the lower branches so the tree sits comfort- ably in the pot.

To make Santa's hat, wrap the red felt around the top of the tree into a floppy cone and secure with safety pins. Roll a small ball of stuffing and attach to the end of the hat with safety pins. To make the belt, wrap the black felt strip around the middle of the tree, and secure it with safety pins on the back side. (Depending on the girth of the tree, you may have to tighten Santa's belt.) Once the hat and belt are in place, press generous handfuls of stuffing into Santa's broad face

continued

to make a snowy white beard. Stretch and shape the batting, pushing it onto the needles to keep it in place.

Hang the 2 blue balls for Santa's twinkling eyes, and a big red ornament for his nose. To make Santa's suit, fill the space from the shoulders down and around the belt with the red ornaments.

No Santa Claus? How ridiculous, you can say! Now that you have created your Santa tree, you might be inspired to make him an annual tradition.

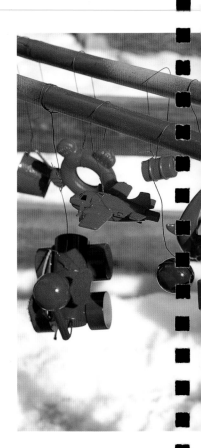

Paint the Toys Red

A can of red spray paint and a bunch of cheap objects are all you need to make inexpensive ornaments for the Santa Tree. Use 24-gauge wire to hang almost any object, from dried miniature pinecones to plastic anteaters, from a clothesline or a horizontal stick. Cover the ground with newspaper, and coat each toy with red enamel spray paint. If you don't like spray paint, invite some elves over for a painting party and use latex paint. Allow the ornaments to dry thoroughly before handling them. Decide what looks good painted red and what does not. Use the rejects on the Tree of Misfit Toys (see page 41).

Frosty the Snow Tree

You will need:
1 bushy tree, 6 to 8 feet tall,
    in a heavy-duty tree
    stand
garden clippers
snow
scissors
1 piece black felt, about
    12 inches square
1 wooden stick, chopstick,
    or dowel about
    12 inches long
hot glue gun
1 piece orange felt,
    12 inches square
1 big scarf or 1 yard thick
    fabric such as felt or
    flannel
3 to 5 silver or blue
    Christmas balls,
    with hangers
pencil
2 pieces heavy black con-
    struction paper, each
    30 by 36 inches
utility knife
1 pipe
1 broom

Frosty, a jolly, happy soul, had a corncob pipe and two eyes made out of coal. But you can make Frosty using things around your house. If a magic hat can't be found, we'll tell you how to make one that will make him dance around.

You'll need to dream up a white Christmas to make Frosty's head out of snow. And because his head is very heavy, you'll need to secure the tree with a heavy-duty tree stand for extra support.

☆ Place the tree on a flat spot, and secure it if needed (see "Giving Frosty a Little Extra Support," page 35). Use the garden clippers to clip away the top branches, leaving the apex of the trunk exposed, like a stake.

To make the head, pack snow into a tight ball about 1 foot in diameter. Gently skewer the snowball onto the tip of the apex. Pack and add snow to the snowball head until it's about 1½ feet in diameter, or until it matches the scale of your tree.

To make the eyes, using scissors, cut out two 4-inch squares from the black felt and press them onto the head (felt sticks to snow as though it were Velcro). Use snow to cover the edges and soften the corners. Cut 5 or 6 smaller pieces of black felt, each about 3 inches square. Press these felt pieces onto

continued

the head to create a jaunty, crooked smile. To make the nose, dot the length of the dowel with hot glue and place it on the edge of the square of orange felt. Roll the dowel up in the felt to create a carrot-like cone, and secure the edge of the felt in place with a drop of hot glue. Insert the nose into the head above the mouth. Wrap the scarf or fabric around Frosty's neck, tie once, and hang the Christmas balls down Frosty's front to look like buttons.

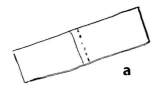 **a** **b**  **c**

To make Frosty's magic hat, use a pencil to draw a circle 30 inches in diameter on one sheet of the construction paper. Use scissors to cut the circle out. This will be the hat's brim. Cut the second sheet of construction paper in half lengthwise (a). Glue the short sides of the 2 pieces together to make a cylinder about 15 inches in diameter (b). Center the cylinder on the brim, and use the pencil to trace it's contour on the brim (c). With a utility knife, make 8 equally spaced cuts through the circle you traced on the brim, giving you 16 pie-shaped flaps (d).

Bend the flaps upward at the edge of the circle. Place the tube back on top of the brim, and hot-glue the flaps to the inside of the tube to secure it to the brim (e). Let the hat dry completely before putting it on Frosty. (You may have to add or subtract snow from Frosty's head to make the hat fit.)

Give him his pipe and broom and then run and have some fun, before he melts away!

d   e

Giving Frosty a Little Extra Support: Because Frosty's head might be a little heavy, you can give him some extra support using stakes and wire. To secure an 8-foot tree, for example, wrap 3 separate lengths of 24-gauge wire around the trunk about two-thirds of the way up from the base of the tree, and then tie them off, leaving at least 6 feet of wire trailing from each one. Use a hammer and stakes to tie down each wire about 2 feet away from the base of the tree. Wiggle the tree to test for stability.

Starry, Starry Night

You will need:
1 large tree, about 8 feet tall, in a tree stand
about 2 yards black or green felt
incandescent black light-bulbs, preferably in clip-on lamps, or a string of black Christmas lights (see note)
pencil
1 piece white foam core, 32 by 40 inches and about ¼ inch thick
utility knife
30 to 40 pieces floral wire, each approximately 9 to 12 inches long
10 Styrofoam balls, 3 to 5 inches in diameter
fluorescent paint
paintbrushes

Celebrate Christmas in space with this glowing tree hung with glimmering planets, brightly blazing rockets, shining stars, and silvery spaceships, in a violet celestial atmosphere. To make the tree, you'll need fluorescent paint and an incandescent black light, both available at select hardware and hobby craft stores.

⭐ Place the tree indoors near an electrical outlet. Wrap the base with the felt. Clip the black-light lamp so that it faces the tree.

To make the stars, rockets, moons, and spaceships, using a pencil, trace each shape onto the foam core. With the utility knife, cut out each shape from the foam core. Insert a piece of floral wire into the edge of each shape and into each of the Styrofoam balls. Generously paint your solar system with fluorescent paint. Let dry, then apply a second coat, let dry again, and apply a third coat. After the ornaments are completely dry, hang them from the tree, using the wires. Turn on the black light and remember, "When you wish upon a star (or planet or spaceship), your dreams come true."

Note: You can sometimes buy strings of black lights at novelty supply stores. If you can't find a black light you can omit it altogether and use glow-in-the-dark paint instead.

Winter Wonderland Welcome

You will need:

5 potted evergreen bushes
(or more, depending on
your space), each 2 to
3 feet tall

6 quart-sized Mason jars

5 strands Christmas lights,
50 lights each (one
strand for each bush)

outdoor extension cord, if
needed

1 pound rice, sand, or pretty
dried beans

6 short, tapered candles

about 60 old or broken
small, colorful Christ-
mas ornaments (see
note)

long-handled kitchen
lighter

"Welcome Christmas, bring your light! Welcome in the cold dark night!" A line of small, lighted conifers in pots welcomes carolers and anyone else who comes to your door. Perk up each pot with a circlet of snow, or slip them into sparkly containers such as shiny galvanized buckets.

☆ Place the potted conifers in a line down your steps or along your walkway, alternating them with Mason jars until you have the composition you like. Gathering the cords at the back, wrap each tree with one string of lights, leaving a tail long enough to power the next one. (The cords will connect in a chain; wrap one tree, trail the extra cord over to the next tree, plug the next string into it, and so on.) Attach the extension cord to the last connected string, if needed, to reach the outlet.

After each tree has been wrapped with lights, pour an inch of rice, sand, or beans into each Mason jar. In each prepared jar, set a candle and arrange about 10 shiny, reflective ornaments. Use a kitchen lighter to illuminate the candles. Plug in the Christmas lights and welcome your guests to take a walk in your winter wonderland.

Note: Use old or broken ornaments in the jars as the melted candle wax will make it hard to reuse your ornaments.

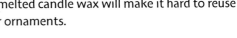

The Little Tree That Could

Not every tree can be the most handsome, but
with a little love, any tree can be a part of your
Christmas. Here's a sweet little tree that Charlie
Brown would certainly appreciate.

A Tree of Misfit Toys

You will need:
1 tree, any size or shape, in
   a sturdy tree stand
collection of broken and/or
   misfit toys, such as
   stuffed animals, doll
   heads, red-nosed rein-
   deer, and misunder-
   stood elves, in various
   shapes, colors, and sizes
wire cutters or sturdy
   scissors
22- to 24-gauge flexible
   wire
hot glue gun
ornament hooks

Whether you have a choo-choo with square
wheels, a cowboy who rides an ostrich, or an ele-
phant with spots, give your misfit toys a home!
In this lovely tree, all your toys are welcome. To
create your tree, begin by placing the largest toys
first, hanging them one by one from biggest to
smallest.

☆ Place the tree indoors or outdoors.
Perch the larger toys and stuffed animals on
sturdy branches. For the medium-sized toys,
use wire cutters to cut 8- to 10-inch pieces
of wire and wrap a piece around each toy
before attaching it to the tree. For the small
toys, hot-glue ornament hooks onto them
and hang them on the tree.

Make-a-Wish Tree

You will need:
1 kiddie wading pool, 3 to
    4 feet in diameter, or a
    galvanized laundry
    bucket, at least 2 feet in
    diameter (large enough
    to fit the tree stand)
1 tree, about 6 feet tall, in
    a sturdy tree stand
hole punch
25 to 30 red plastic cups
30 strings Mardi Gras or
    other plastic beads,
    each about 6 inches
    long, or colorful pipe
    cleaners
newspaper
spray adhesive
red and silver glitter
15 large candy canes
30 silver Christmas balls
    and bells, with hangers

Invite the neighborhood to make a wish. Close your eyes, toss coins into glittery red cups, and then wait for your wish to come true. A pool below catches the missed coins. If you want to be an angel, collect the change and give it to your favorite charity. Add a few bells to ting-a-ling when you earn your angel wings.

☆ Pick a good place outside for your wishing tree. If you have deep snow, dig the pool or bucket into it. Place the tree in the pool or bucket.

To make the wish cups, use the hole punch to punch a hole just under the lip of a cup. Punch an identical hole on the opposite side. If you are using a string of beads, push the first bead of the strand through one of the holes from the outside in. Push the last bead of the strand through the other hole from the out-side in. Repeat to make the remaining wish cups. Cover a surface with newspaper. Invert the cups, spray the bottoms and sides with adhesive, and sprinkle with glitter, catching the excess on the newspaper.

Hang the wish cups at different levels on the tree, placing a few near the bottom for players who need a little help. Hang the candy canes and silver balls and bells from the tree.

Your Family Tree

You will need:

1 tree, any size, preferably with widely spaced branches, in a sturdy tree stand
tree skirt
removable double-stick tape
family photos
sheets of 9-by-12-inch construction paper in assorted colors (1 sheet per 4 or 5 photos)
color copy machine
laminating machine
scissors, pinking shears, or deckle-edge scissors
hole punch
permanent marker
ornament hooks or narrow ribbon, cut into 6-inch lengths

Trimming the tree with family photographs becomes a time to share stories of moments past. Remember that crazy Christmas party when Arthur and Betty Sue drank all the eggnog and did a jitterbug on the kitchen table? How about the time Grandpa Joe hauled home a Yule log so big it wouldn't fit through the front door?

Old photos are very delicate, so we made our ornaments using laminated color copies instead. The lamination preserves the image and makes it stiff enough to hang. Plus, you can make duplicate copies to give as gifts. Be sure to write the names of your family members on the back of each photo, and include a funny caption or quote. You can find lamination and copy machines in most copy stores.

⭐ Set up the tree indoors and arrange the skirt around the base.

Use the double-stick tape to stick assorted family photos onto the sheets of colored paper, leaving at least 1 inch of space between the photos. Make a color copy of each sheet of paper, and then laminate each copy.

Using scissors, pinking shears, or deckle-edge scissors, cut out each photo, leaving a pretty border around the edges. Punch a hole in the top of each photo, using the hole punch.

continued

Using the permanent marker, pen the name, date, occasion, and even a funny story on the back of each photo. Hang the photos on the tree, using the ornament hooks or lengths of pretty ribbon. Put great-grandma and -grandpa at the top and work down the tree to all the kids, cousins, cats, and dogs!

North Star Supernova

O star of wonder, star of night! With a tree as bright as the North Star, you might find three kings (and maybe Santa and Rudolph) standing at your door bearing gifts of gold, frankincense, and myrrh. To make our tree as bright as a supernova, we wrapped 1500 lights around it, until it "exploded" into the night. Twine extensions guide additional strings of lights upward and outward from the core, creating arching flares.

Paradise Tree

1 lovely bare deciduous or evergreen tree

collection of natural objects such as moss, small stones, lichen-covered sticks, palm fronds, aromatic branches and dried flowers, and leaves

wire cutters or sturdy scissors

20-gauge metal wire or floral wire

waxed linen thread or twine in a neutral color

assortment of brightly colored fruits such as oranges, apples, cranberries, pears, and limes, and vegetables such as colorful squashes

long, sturdy stick with a notch in one end

During the Middle Ages, the Paradise Tree represented the Tree of Knowledge in the miracle play about Adam and Eve. This Paradise Tree is decorated with fruits and vegetables, including pears (the partridge is hiding here, somewhere) and other bright, natural objects. It's a humble but beautiful sight for holiday hikers, birds, and squirrels as well.

☆ To hang branches, dried flowers, and other light objects from the tree, using wire cutters, cut 8-inch lengths of wire, wrap one end around an object, and attach it to the tree with the other end. To hang smooth objects such as rocks, wrap a piece of waxed linen thread around the center and tie it off, leaving a small knot. Then loop a small length of wire under the knot and hang the object on the tree.

To hang fruit and vegetables, twist a loop of wire around the stem if there is a sturdy one, or poke a 6- to 8-inch length of wire through the fruit near the stem and twist the ends to close it into a loop.

To hang ornaments high in the tree, use a long stick with a notch in one end. Make the wire loop long enough to engage the branch. Using the notch, lift the ornament above the desired branch, snag the wire on the branch, and leave the ornament behind.

Sugarplum Tree

You will need:

1 small artificial tree with lights, about 1½ feet tall

tray or platter

scissors

¼ pound gummy or sour ribbons, or other long, pliable candies such as licorice whips

1 or 2 pounds assorted colorful wrapped hard candies, including small candy canes and lollipops

ornament hooks

5 to 10 marzipan fruits

1 bag cotton candy (optional)

jelly beans

When visions of sugarplums dance in your head, serve this tree on a tray to all your favorite nut-crackers. We made our tree skirt out of cotton candy and adorned it with candy canes and balls of marzipan. Add other goodies from the King-dom of Sweets, like nuts, macaroons, and candied fruits.

An artificial tree prestrung with lights and sturdy wire branches is perfect for holding candy. Because this dreamy tree will attract the Mouse King (and other pesky guests), it is best to serve it soon after you make it.

☆ Place your tree on a colorful tray or bright platter. Using scissors, cut the gummy or sour ribbons into strips 6 to 8 inches long. Tie the strips around the tree branches like little ribbons, distributing them evenly around the tree. Hook the candy canes over the branches, and use the ornament hooks to hang the remaining candy and the marzipan fruit until your tree is loaded with sweets. Surround the tree with a swath of cotton candy, and scatter jelly beans on top.

Note: This tiny tree is a kid-friendly addition to any party. Give the children stockings and let them pick their own party favors.

A Tiny Tree for Tiny Tim

When Scrooge made Bob Cratchit work overtime, Bob used all of Scrooge's office supplies to decorate a tree branch for Tiny Tim's tiny desktop. You can use any type of evergreen cutting with a woody stem. If your tree is sturdy enough, top it with a paper clip star. Self-adhesive dots are available in most office-supply stores.

⭐ Peel away any foliage from the lower woody end of the branch to make a trunk. Use a pair of scissors to puncture a small hole in the eraser. Insert the trunk into the eraser, and twist until the branch is secure.

To make a garland, stick the adhesive dots, back to back, onto the thread. Drape the garland around the tree. Embellish the Post-it pads with a few extra dots, and put them under the tree for miniature presents. And remember the words of Tiny Tim, "God bless us, every one!"

Peace on Earth Bonsai

A Japanese legend holds that if you fold one thousand origami cranes you will be granted a wish. The crane has come to be a symbol of the wish for peace on Earth—an especially appropriate wish at Christmas. We made a miniature version as a reminder of that wish.

chapter three

Crafty Christmas Trees

If you can't find the tree you love, love the tree you make. In this chapter you will discover that a Christmas tree can be crafted out of just about anything, from a houseplant to a pile of sand. Let yourself go wild! When you are in the desert, hang your ornaments on a barrel cactus. Stranded on a tropical isle? Drape tinsel on that royal palm. You don't need a pine to get into the spirit of Christmas. Bring the Christmas spirit everywhere you go.

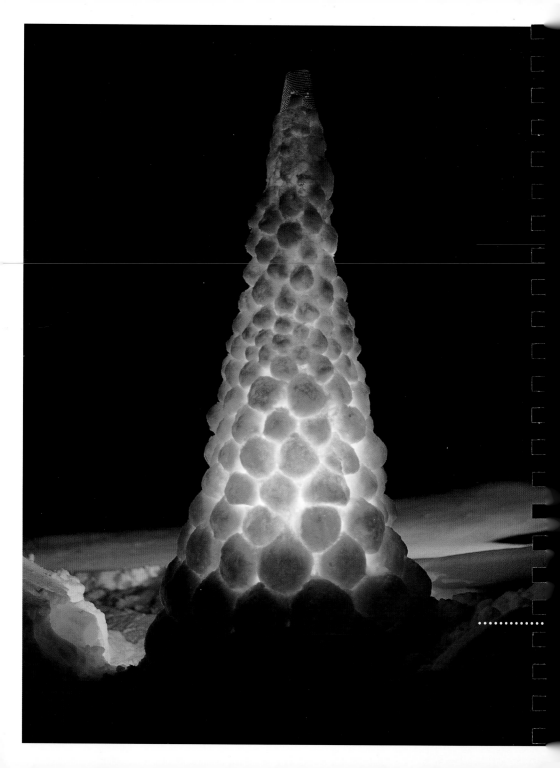

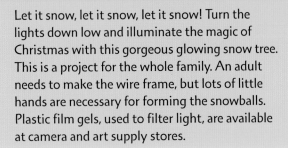

Let It Snow

You will need:

outdoor extension cord
4 thin wooden poles or
stakes, each approxi-
mately 6 feet long
30 pieces of 22- to 24-
gauge wire, each about
6 inches long
wire cutters or tinsnips
roll of galvanized 1/4-inch-
mesh hardware cloth,
20 feet long by 30
inches wide
snow
outdoor-rated utility lamp
with 100-watt bulb
1 green plastic film gel

Let it snow, let it snow, let it snow! Turn the lights down low and illuminate the magic of Christmas with this gorgeous glowing snow tree. This is a project for the whole family. An adult needs to make the wire frame, but lots of little hands are necessary for forming the snowballs. Plastic film gels, used to filter light, are available at camera and art supply stores.

☆ Select a snowy spot for your tree within reach of your extension cord. Position the 4 poles in a circle, 2 1/2 feet apart, burying the ends about 1 foot deep into the snow. Use wire to bind the tops of the poles into a teepee at the top.

Using wire cutters, cut the piece of hardware cloth in half lengthwise, creating two 10-foot lengths. Attach one corner of one length to the top of the teepee with an anchor wire. Allow the cloth to spiral down around the poles from the top, forming half the cone. Attach the cloth to the poles every 12 inches with pieces of wire, and also attach it to itself where it crosses. At the base, fold any extra cloth flat to the ground and cover with snow. Repeat with the remaining half of the cloth, spiraling and securing it in the same way, to complete the cone. In the back of the structure, at ground level, use wire cutters to cut a hole large enough to slip in

continued

the light later. Smooth and tightly pack at least 1 foot of snow around the base to secure the cone and create a foundation for the snowballs.

Ring the base of the tree with hard-packed 12-inch snowballs, leaving the light hole exposed. Stack slightly smaller snowballs on top of the first ring, leaning them slightly into the mesh. Stack and build snowballs tightly to the top, gradually decreasing their size.

Cover the light with the green film gel, place the light inside the base of the cone, and plug it in. Flick the switch on a few minutes after dusk, and enjoy the green glow.

Santa Cactus

You will need:
scissors
1 piece red felt, 6 inches
    square
1 Old Man of Mexico
    cactus (*Cephalocereus
    senilis*)
hot glue gun
1 white pipe cleaner

A cactus makes a prickly Santa even the Grinch could love. A small, red hat will turn your *Cephalocereus senilis,* or Old Man of Mexico, into a jolly desert Santa.

☆ To make Santa's hat, use the scissors to cut out a circle of red felt about 4 inches in diameter. Cut a slit in the circle, from the edge to the center point, and overlap the resulting flaps until the circle forms a cone. Size the cone to fit your cactus, and then secure the flaps with the glue gun. Trim the bottom edge of the hat with the white pipe cleaner, cutting it to size and hot-gluing it in place. Make a pompom from a snippet of pipe cleaner and attach it to the top of the hat with a dab of hot glue. Gently place the hat on your "Old Man."

To complete the scene, surround Santa with cactus "elves" and a mini sack of desert presents, if you like.

A Tree for Tinsel Town

Shining with thousands of silvery strands, this sparkly tree is as glamorous as any star in Hollywood. Surround this tree with blinking multicolored lights for a New Year's Eve disco dance party.

Sparkly Icicle Forest

You will need:
gloves
icicles
glitter, in assorted colors
newspaper
pipe cleaners, in assorted
    colors

A forest of frozen thunderbolts becomes a winter wonderland perfect for teeny elves. You can make this little icicle grove on a small snowbank or against a snow-laden windowsill. While little hands can do the decorating, adults should use extreme care and gloves when pulling and placing the icicles.

☆ Wearing gloves, carefully break icicles from a roof or other overhang. Still wearing gloves, decorate your icicles using one of the following techniques:

Option 1: Shake glitter over the icicles, catching the extra on a piece of newspaper. (Never litter with glitter.)

Option 2: Twist a pipe cleaner around your index finger to form a spiral. Remove the spiral, stretch it out a bit, and slip it over the tip of an icicle.

Turn the icicles pointed-side up, and plant them in a snowbank or on a snow-covered windowsill. Repeat until you have grown a forest fit for an ice queen.

Jingle Fish Tree

You will need:
scissors
plastic seaweed
hot glue gun
1 small, flat rock or tiny
    flower frog
colorful string, 20 inches
    long
15 to 20 tiny beads
gold or silver foil
clear marbles

Everyone needs a little Christmas cheer, even your finned friends. What fish wouldn't like a fir like this in its living room? You can buy plastic seaweed at most aquarium and pet supply stores.

☆ To make the tree, use scissors to cut the seaweed fronds from their base. Turn the resulting pieces upside down, and hot-glue them together in staggered heights to form a pointed, tree-shaped bundle. Hot-glue this bundle to a small rock or tiny flower frog to give it weight and stability. Wrap the string around the tree in overlapping spirals. Hot-glue plastic beads to the intersections of the string. Cut out a tiny star from the foil and hot-glue it to the top. Submerge your tree in the fishbowl and surround it with marbles.

Christmas at the Beach

You will need:
sand, at the beach of
course!
shovel
1 wooden pole or stake,
about 5 feet long
collection of colorful plastic beach toys, balls,
sunglasses, buckets and
spades, picnic coolers,
and anything else that
would make a great
waterproof decoration
ball of strong twine
scissors
beach towels

When Sandy Claus catches a Christmas morning wave, greet that super surfer with this tree full of treasures. Plastic beach toys make vivid water-proof ornaments, and towels serve as a festive tree skirt. Top your tree with a pinwheel any heat-miser would love. Always make sandcastles as the tide is going out, and work facing the sea in case of big waves.

★ Choose a place to make the sand tree that is safely back from the waves but close enough that the sand is wet. With the shovel dig a small 1-foot-deep hole, stick in the pole, and pack it firmly in place with sand. To keep the toys and other objects from falling off, you will tie them to the pole with twine. Pack sand up and around the pole until you have a huge sand cone. Bury large objects such as beach balls and coolers into the base. Reserve lighter objects, like sunglasses and toy buckets and spades, for the top, where they can be poked in to cover bare spots. Place beach towels around the base of the "tree" to resemble a tree skirt.

Remember to recover your buried treasures and take them home. Keep the beach clean.

It's a Wonderful Life Memory Tree

You will need:
2 eye hooks
wooden plank or old
    cabinet door, about
    30 inches square
picture-hanging wire
pencil
collection of compelling
    odds and ends (see
    introduction)
hot glue gun

Make a tree of tiny treasures and paper ephemera to remind you of special moments in your wonderful life. We made ours using childhood photographs, cancelled stamps and envelopes, ticket stubs from memorable movies, matchboxes from favorite restaurants, plastic toys, dried flowers, beads, a set of jacks, and a Superball. We didn't ask him, but we bet Jimmy Stewart would have included Zuzu's petals and a pair of wings on his Wonderful Life tree. This tree is great for a family collaboration, with built-in history lessons.

☆ Screw in eye hooks on each side of the back of your plank or door. Attach picture-hanging wire by threading through both hooks and twisting together the ends to form a loop. Use a pencil to sketch a tree shape on the front. Arrange your odds and ends within the outlines of your tree shape. Use the bigger items for the bottom of the tree and work your way up to the top, using smaller and smaller items. Once you like your composition, hot-glue each item in place, one at a time. Hang your tree of memories in a place where everyone can see it.

'Twas the Light Before Christmas

You will need:
1 piece heavy green
    construction paper or
    single-weight card-
    board, 24 by 30 inches
scissors
pencil
X-Acto knife
colored tissue paper, or
    translucent plastic such
    as colored cellophane
clear tape
hot glue gun
lamp with existing small
    tapered shade, 6 to
    9 inches in diameter

"'Twas the night before Christmas and all through the house, not a creature was stirring, not even a mouse." By the light of this festive lamp, you can read this famous holiday story to your child, all snug in his or her bed.

☆ Following the diagram, cut a cone shape from the construction paper, using scissors. A cone of a different size will work, but it must fit over your existing lampshade. Use a pencil to draw shapes such as stars and trees, and cut them out using the X-Acto knife. Cover the cutouts with pieces of colored tissue for a stained glass look and tape to secure. Using scissors, fringe the bottom edge of the cone. When the decorations are complete, gently roll the cone up, tape-side in, and glue it securely, using a hot glue gun. Place over the lampshade, click on the light, and see it glow.

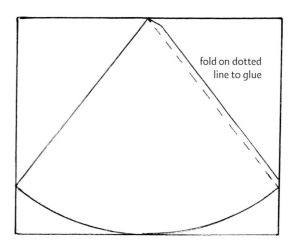

fold on dotted
line to glue

chapter four

Incredible Edible Trees

Feed your tree trimmers with treats shaped like trees. This collection of incredible edibles will delight little sprites and make your guests whistle as they work decorating *your* tree. A tower of Brownie de Noels or Mrs. Claus's Snow Globe Cupcakes served with a cup of Minty Hot Chocolate will have them rocking around the *Tannenbaum!*

Mrs. Claus's Snow Globe Cupcakes

Cupcakes
18 foil cupcake liners
1 package (18.25 ounces)
   plain white cake mix
1 cup milk
3 large eggs
2 tablespoons vegetable oil
2 teaspoons pure vanilla or
   almond extract

Icing
4 ounces cream cheese, at
   room temperature
2 tablespoons unsalted
   butter, at room temperature
1/2 cup confectioners' sugar

Decorations
1 package (6 ounces) shredded sweetened coconut
18 green or white Starburst
   candies or fruit-flavored
   Tootsie Rolls
18 toothpicks
green, red, and white
   sprinkles
18 silver dragées

Makes 18 cupcakes

Eat, Papa! Eat! That is what Mrs. Claus says to Santa every year. Her famous snow globe cupcakes have made Santa the round and jolly character we all know and love. Since Mrs. Claus is very busy, she makes her cupcakes using a cake mix and then whips up a bit of her famous frosting. The tree-shaped toppers are Santa's favorite and are relatively easy to make.

You can make the cupcakes 1 day ahead (leave them unfrosted) and keep them in an airtight container at room temperature.

☆ Preheat the oven to 325°F. Place the foil liners in a muffin tin.

To make the cupcakes, in a large bowl, combine the cake mix, milk, eggs, vegetable oil, and extract. Use a wooden spoon or an electric mixer to beat until smooth. Fill the liners about three-fourths full. Bake the cupcakes in the oven on the middle rack until golden, 15 to 20 minutes. Let cool.

To make the icing, use an electric mixer to beat together the cream cheese, butter, and confectioners' sugar until the icing is fluffy. Using a knife or spatula, spread the icing on the cupcakes. Sprinkle with some of the shredded coconut and set aside.

To make the tree toppers, use your fingers to knead a Starburst or fruit-flavored Tootsie

Roll into a cone shape. Insert a toothpick into the base of the cone and press sprinkles onto the sides to look like ornaments. Repeat with the remaining candy. Top each tree with a silver dragée. Stick a toothpick tree topper into each cupcake.

Nestle the cupcakes onto a cake plate covered in the remaining snowy shredded coconut, and serve.

Brownie de Noel

Brownies
2/3 cup all-purpose flour
1/4 teaspoon salt
1/2 teaspoon baking
    powder
1/3 cup unsalted butter, at
    room temperature
1 cup sugar
2 eggs
2 ounces (2 squares) semi-
    sweet chocolate,
    melted
1 teaspoon pure vanilla
    extract

Decorations
3 candy necklaces
1 small bag candy corn
1/4 cup M&M's or other
    small round chocolates
    and foil-wrapped
    candies

Makes 24 brownies

Kids can decorate this chocolate "tree" with necklace garlands, candy corn "candles," fancy wrapped chocolate packages, and other sweet treats.

⭐ Preheat the oven to 350°F. Grease an 8-inch square pan.

In a medium bowl, whisk together the flour, salt, and baking powder; set aside. In a separate bowl, use an electric mixer to cream the butter and sugar until light and fluffy. Beat in the eggs and chocolate. Mix in the flour mixture. Stir in the vanilla and place in the prepared pan. Place the pan in the oven on the middle rack and bake until set, 20 to 25 minutes. Let cool completely in the pan. Cut into 24 squares.

To make your brownie tree, stack the brownies into a pyramid, and decorate with the candy treats.

Sugary Cookie Trees

Cookies
2 2/3 cups all-purpose flour
1 teaspoon baking powder
1/2 teaspoon salt
1 cup (2 sticks) unsalted butter, at room temperature
1 cup packed brown sugar
1 large egg
2 teaspoons pure vanilla extract
Christmas cookie cutters, each 3 to 4 inches, floured

Icing
2 cups confectioners' sugar
1 egg white
1/2 teaspoon fresh lemon juice
food coloring
4 disposable pastry bags

Decorations
red and green sprinkles
silver dragées

Makes 3 dozen cookies

Give your guests some trees to taste while they trim the tree. This simple sugar-cookie dough is easy to make, but you could just as easily use ready-made dough. You can find great cookie cutters at cooking stores and vintage shops.

☆ To make the cookies, in a small mixing bowl whisk together the flour, baking powder, and salt. Set aside. In a large mixing bowl, use an electric mixer to beat together the butter and sugar until fluffy. Beat in the egg and vanilla until smooth. Add the flour mixture and mix until combined. Turn the dough out onto a lightly floured surface and knead gently for 1 minute. Shape the dough into a 1/2-inch-thick rectangle. Cut it into 4 equal pieces; wrap in plastic wrap and refrigerate for at least 3 hours and up to 1 day. Let the dough soften slightly at room temperature before rolling it out.

Position a rack in the center of the oven and preheat the oven to 325°F. Working with one piece of dough at a time, roll the dough out on a lightly floured surface to a thickness of about 1/8 inch, lifting and turning the dough often and dusting the surface very lightly with flour to prevent sticking. Using the floured cutters, cut out cookies. Pull the excess dough away from around the cookies. Transfer the cookies to a buttered baking sheet, spacing them 1 inch apart.

continued

(If you will be using the cookies as hanging ornaments, use a drinking straw to make a small hole near the top of each cookie.) Gently reroll the dough scraps and cut out more cookies. Transfer to the same baking sheet. Bake the cookies until they are light brown, about 11 minutes. Let cool 5 minutes on the sheet. Transfer the cookies to a rack; let cool.

To make the icing, in a large bowl, combine the sugar, egg white, and lemon juice. With a wooden spoon, mix the ingredients together until the icing is thickened and smooth, about 2 minutes. Place 1/2 cup of the frosting into each of 4 small bowls, and add drops of food coloring to the bowls, tinting each a different color. (The icing will keep for 2 days in an airtight container in the refrigerator. Before using, stir with a fork, adding a very small amount of water if necessary.)

To decorate the cookies, using a pastry brush or a small spatula, spread frosting on the cookies; set the cookies aside until the frosting is dry, about 30 minutes. Cut a small tip from the end of a disposable pastry bag and fill the bag with 1 color of the frosting. Repeat with the remaining pastry bags, filling each with 1 color of frosting. Pipe decorations onto the frosted cookies. Add sprinkles and dragée ornaments. Let the cookies stand until the decorations are firm and dry, at least 4 hours. To make a forest diorama, plant each tree cookie in a dollop of frosting.

Minty Hot Chocolate

¼ cup unsweetened cocoa
3 tablespoons sugar
salt
½ cup water
4 cups milk
3 or 4 drops peppermint
   extract
whipped cream
6 sprigs fresh mint
6 candy canes

Makes 6 servings

This minty hot chocolate is a sweet, rich ending to any holiday party.

⭐ Mix the cocoa, sugar, and salt with the water in a medium saucepan, and boil gently for 2 minutes. Add the milk and heat slowly just to the boiling point. Beat well with a whisk and flavor with the peppermint extract. Pour into cups and top each with a dollop of whipped cream. Plant a mint sprig and a candy cane in each mug.

about the authors

Peter Cole, Frankie Frankeny, and Leslie Jonath have collaborated on many kooky projects including *Snowmen: Creatures, Crafts, and Other Winter Projects* published by Chronicle Books.

Peter is a sculptor whose work has appeared in national and international shows. He lives in Santa Barbara, California.

Frankie is a San Francisco–based photographer and author whose work has appeared in magazines and books including The *Star Wars* cookbooks, *After-Dinner Drinks, On Rice, The Christmas Cookie Book, Sorbets and Ice Creams,* and *The Art of Chocolate,* all published by Chronicle Books.

Leslie is an editor and a writer living in San Francisco. She is the author of *Postmark Paris: A Little Album of Memories; Makin' Waves: Fun for Kids in the Tub; Splish Splash: Recipes for the Bath* and *Stamp It! The Ultimate Stamp Collecting Activity Book,* all published by Chronicle Books.

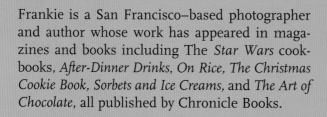